At the Park

**Written and photographed by
Donna L. Cuevas Roeder**

People read at the park.

People sit at the park.

4

People ride bikes

at the park.

People go fishing

at the park.

People play at the park.

People walk in the park.

People also eat

at the park.